ERIN LORIMER

"The only thing better than *Fire Up!* is being Fired Up by Jan in person. If you are interested in learning how to go from zero to your sixth million from a woman who's done it—AND can show and tell YOU how to do it—read Jan's book and listen to her tapes. In fact, listen to them at least once a month for the next year. When you do, you'll know what Jan knows, and that will change your life for the better forever!"

—John Milton Fogg, Author
Founder of Upline and Network
Marketing Lifestyles magazine

"I keep *Fire Up!* with me where ever I go so that I have Jan's spirit with me always. This book is my favorite way to start and end my day. *Fire Up!* keeps my passion for my business ablaze. I have been in Network Marketing for years. I have never been so Fired Up as I have been since connecting with Jan Ruhe."

—Cathy Walker, Gold Sales Director
Discovery Toys, Canada

"In this book, Jan gives you the feeling that she is talking only to you. In *Fire Up!* she spoke to me and changed my life. She is a close and dear friend and from knowing her my passion for being the best I can be has grown 100 fold. Read this book, it's a must have for your organization."

—Sue DuPreez, Bahati Adventures South Africa

"When you want to get fired up, locked in, and building your dreams — turn to Jan Ruhe!"

—Randy Gage, Author

"In *Fire Up!*, Jan Ruhe provides us with the essential tools, wisdom and inner fire critical to achieving outrageous, on-fire success as a top networking leader and money-earner. Make the concepts in the book your own and watch people show up en masse to watch you burn with the charisma and passion that will attract the world to you!"

Joe Rubino, Author

D0994122

"*Fire Up!* was the first book I read to explore just how to build an incredible business. I did it and you can too. Next, get everyone in your successline reading it too. Feel the power of Jan's words and wisdom. Reading Fire Up over and over has changed my life."

—Cathy Barber
Canada

"*Fire Up!* is a must read. When you decide to reach your dreams, wild horses can't stop you. By setting goals that are shared in this book, you will ignite your passion and go for your wildest dreams. No doubt about it, if you are ready for a paycheck instead of a playcheck, this book will fire you up! It did my organization, for years!"

—Kathy Smith, Gold Sales Director
Discovery Toys, USA

"*Fire Up!* is a book that I recommend for all Network Marketers to have out on their desk and read on a daily basis to stay fired up! Motivation comes from within, staying Fired Up! forever is easy when you read this book! I love it!"

—Nicky Horkings
Top distributor USANA-Australia

"Rare is the word that comes to mind when I think of Jan Ruhe and Fire Up! A rare talent...a rare gifting...a rare level of success in this industry...and a rare compassion for people...Fire Up! is a rare gem and gift to us all on this business, and I believe that you can tap into the incredible SuccessFire of Jan's with her words and HOT pearls of wisdom, and create anything in your life you want, and set your own success on Fire with Fire Up!

—Doug Firebaugh, PassionFire Industries

"*Fire Up!* is one of the few books written by a real networker that truly knows Network Marketing. I recommend it to everyone who is doing this business seriously!"

—Sandy Martinez, Emerald Executive
Nuskin, Phillipines/Manila

FIRE UP!

by Jan Ruhe

www.janruhe.com

**This is the U.K. Printing
By B.I.D.S. Supplies
in conjunction with
Proteus Press**

Fire Up!
Copyright © 1995 by Jan Ruhe

This publication is designed to provide accurate and authoritative information in regards to the subject matter covered. It is sold with the understanding that the author is not engaged in rendering legal, accounting, or other professional service. If legal advice or other expert assistance is required, the services of a competent professional person should be sought. From a Declaration of Principles jointly adopted by a Committee of the American Bar Association and a Committee of Publishers.

This book contains Jan Ruhe's opinions and personal experiences. Her opinions do not necessarily reflect those of her company, or any persons living or dead unless directly stated.

Copyright © 1995 by Jan Ruhe
Published by JR Productions
www.janruhe.com
Telephone: IN USE, 1-970-972-3010
First Printing January, 1994; Second Printing April 1995;
    Third Printing April, 1998; Fourth Printing, March, 2001
Printed in the USA by Proteus Press
This is the U.K. printing by B.I.D.S. Supplies in conjunction with Proteus Press
Cover Design by Christine Crane; photo by Dave Marlow–Aspen Colorado

10 9 8 7 6 5 4

"All successful people have something to prove."

—Jan Ruhe

NEVER GIVE UP

Dedications

To my children, Clayton, Ashley, and Sarah White–the three brightest lights in my lifetime–and to all those who have contributed to my life and my children's lives, thank you and *Fire Up!*

Life is not what has happened in the past. That's history. Life is what is happening this very minute. Life truly is a dance: sometimes you lead, sometimes you follow–just learn as you go.

"I do believe there are Angels here amongst us."

–Jan Ruhe

Decide to Be Fired Up!

Use every email and call you make
Every conversation you have
Every meeting you hold or attend
To let everyone know your dreams and desires
Let people know of your vision of what you expect
Fire Up! others around you
Fire Up! and forgive those who have hurt you
Fire Up! your vocabulary and choose your words carefully
You are a powerful person
Spread the fire of desire
Radiate your passion
Believe in yourself
Concentrate on what you do right
No human is perfect, forgive yourself
You can't change the past
Focus on your goals, your dreams and your hopes
Believe in miracles, expect them do not be surprised by them
Come to the table of plenty, there is a place set for you.
Your success will be served on a silver platter.
Stay Fired up no matter what.
The day you decide is the day that your life will change for the
better forever.
Decide to stay Fired Up! for life!
-Jan Ruhe

The Optimist Creed

Commit yourself:

To be so strong that nothing can disturb your peace of
mind.

To talk health, happiness, and prosperity to every person
you meet.

To make all of your friends feel that there is something
wonderful in them.

To look at the sunny side of everything and make your
optimism come true.

To think only of the best, to work only for the best, and
expect only the best.

To be just as enthusiastic about the success of others as
you are about your own.

To forget the mistakes of the past and press on to the
greater achievements of the future.

To wear a cheerful countenance at all times and give
every living creature you meet a smile.

To give so much time to the improvement of yourself
that you have no time to criticize others.

To be too large for worry, too noble for anger, too strong
for fear, and too happy to permit the presence of
trouble.

—Optimist International

Table of Contents

The Fired Up! Pledge

The decision is made, I am Fired Up! for life!
I will become the best I can be no matter what!
It's time that I ignite the Power of Me!
No longer will I wait to unleash the Giant within!

I deserve greatness, I will not hold back,
I will from today on not listen to those who tell me I can't,
And will embrace only those who tell me I can!

I do not need to ever be worried that I can't succeed!
I will never give in to those who do not lift me up!
I am Fired Up! for life, there is no stopping me now!

I listen to those who pull me up and cheer me on, I am not
motivated from without but from within!
I will press on into the future with gusto!
I will talk wealth, health and happiness to everyone I meet!
I will follow the pioneers and seek out those living the lifestyle I
want!
I am aggressively pursuing the lifestyle I deserve!
I won't quit until I have achieved my goals, watch out!

I will not manage others, I will lead others!
I will manage myself starting today so that I can lead others to a
fantastic, fabulous future with the fire of desire!

I am determined to stay Fired Up! no matter what life brings me!
I will not give in to anyone who will not lead me or follow me!
I am willing to work on myself for as long as it takes,
I will read more, listen to more tapes and will believe in myself
until I achieve my goals!
I know that from today forward I am only going for greatness!
Please know that I am Fired Up! and am starting over and from
today on I will not let anyone, any person or any situation knock
me, rock me or devour my hunger for my lofty dreams!

I am Fired Up!

Prologue
Jan Ruhe is My Best Friend
By Sarah Janell White, 1994

MY BEST FRIEND . . .

. . . is one who comes in when the rest of the world has gone out.

. . . is one who stands by my side to help defend my rights and pride.

She is truly a friend.

She was there the first time I cried, laughed, discovered my thumb, ate, drank, and crawled.

She watched me walk, run, and ride a bike.

She planned all my birthday parties and watched as I walked into school for the first time. Through soccer games, piano recitals, ice skating, Brownie Scouts, tap, ballet, and jazz recitals, gymnastics and twirling competitions, cheerleading camps, and drill team performances, she always sat patiently.

She watched me fall in love for the first time and held my hand through all of the heartaches.

She kissed away my tears and bandaged my scraped knees.

She smiled when I smiled, and laughed when I laughed. Through all of the boyfriends and best friends, she has always been there.

She bought me my first lipstick, my first high heels, and my first car.

We give so little when we give our possessions to others. It's when we give ourselves that we truly give. She gave so much when she had so little to give.

She was a single parent with three children under ten years old, but she made it.

She **never gave up.** "Quit" was a word that never crossed her mind.

She held her head up, pressing on in her quest for success.

She taught me the meanings of the words "inspiration" and "respect." For this lady, I hold the utmost respect and wish nothing but the best.

For years she stayed up until two o'clock in the morning returning phone calls to the west coast, filing, filling out paper work, reading, listening to tapes, planning, thinking, and working so she could to put food on the table for us. Somehow, we never missed out on anything; we always participated in sports and activities and had the nicest clothes. Sometimes I would go in her office and find her working in the middle of the night. I'd pull in my pillow and blanket and sleep right beside her on the floor while she worked.

All the work she did to keep her head above water, to survive, has now paid off.

She began by studying the pros, reading and mirroring each and every thing they suggested to succeed.

She used their words and actions, building her own business day by day.

She set up an office in the dining room so that she could work at home while watching us grow up.

She had no support from anyone, but something inside her forced her to go on.

Nineteen years later, her business, a Network Marketing company, is one of the largest and most successful. Over seven thousand women and men bring in to her national organization millions of dollars in sales every month.

She travels around the country giving inspirational seminars, sharing with people her success story, how she made it to the top.

She has taught me so much in life, especially to depend on no one but yourself for what you want out of life. What you put into life is what you get out, and I truly believe that.

She is a working mother but she's always been there for us, no matter how trying the times, and she will always be there for us.

How lucky my brother, Clayton, sister, Ashley, and I are to have such a role model—my mother—my best friend, Jan Ruhe.

Bill Brown made a million—Bill Brown, think of that!
A boy, you remember, as poor as a rat.
He hoed for the neighbors, did jobs by the day,
But Bill made a million, or more they say.
You can't understand it? Well neither could I,
And then I remembered, and now I know why:
The bell might be ringin', the dinner horn blow,
But Bill always hoed to the end of the row.
Bill worked for my father, you maybe recall;
He wasn't a wonder, not that, not that at all;
He couldn't out-hoe me, or cover more ground,
Or hoe any cleaner, or beat me around;
In fact, I was better in one way that I know,
One toot from the kitchen, and home I would go;
But Bill always hoed to the end of the row.
We used to get hungry out there in the corn.
When you talk about music, what equals a horn,
A horn yellin' dinner, tomatoes and beans,
And pork and potatoes and gravy and greens?
I ain't blamin' no one for quittin' on time.
To stop at the whistle, that ain't any crime,
But as for the million, well this much I know:
That Bill Brown always hoed to the end of the row!

—Author Unknown

There may be better success formulas than the ability to finish the job, but I don't know just what they are. Any woman or man shows a great character strength when she/he keeps on and stays Fired Up in a good cause in spite of distractions, difficulties, and other unforeseen events. If you mess up in life, you can always start all over again. It's never too late to Fire Up! Just do it!

Fire Up!

So Fire Up! everybody!

I'm so excited to share with you some thoughts that will help you be the very best and most fired up person that you can be—this next year . . . this next month . . . this next day . . . this next minute!

I'm so fired up to share this information with you! And here's why:

So many people have called me and asked,

"Jan, what did you do? How is it that you've become a millionaire through MLM? How did you build such a big Network Marketing organization? What are some of the secrets that have worked for you?"

Well, before you read any further, let me answer that question right up front:

What I have done is exactly, precisely everything that's in this book—every, single thing. Throughout this book just check off what you accomplish!

This isn't theory or concepts you're about to read. It's my life! Now please understand, not everything that I do, and not every single thing you'll be learning about in this book, will necessarily work for you. But you know what? If you get just that one idea that pushes you over the top, it will be worth it.

I'm not a motivator—you can be your own best motivator. I'm just hoping to be one of your inspirational and educational coaches.

I am not a cheerleader. All I can tell you is that I've done it, and it's worked. It will work for you, too—even if all you use is one solitary key idea.

When you decide to become a student and look for champions to study and model, you will start to turn every moment into a learning opportunity. Reach out for people who will become your teachers. If there could be a Ring of Honor in the middle of America, these are the people, the teachers whom I'd put in that special Ring.

Tom Hopkins, my mentor. After I sat in my first seminar with him, my life transformed. I went to seven of his one-day seminars. His exact words changed my life.

My other mentor is Jim Rohn. He's a philosopher. He has taught me more than anyone else about life, about taking the time to make it precious and giving every moment the greatest value that it can possibly have. I've taken my children to his seminars.

Next, John Milton Fogg, the founder of Upline™ and a Contributing Editor for *Success* magazine. John has also become my friend. Who would you have in your Ring of Honor? Whomever they are, find them as soon as you can. Learn passionately from what all your mentors say. Start reading everything they've written, listen to all their tapes, watch their videos, attend their seminars over and over again. Use their words—listen to what they have to say about their own experiences and learn from them . . . learn everything from them! You, too, can be a champion. There's no reason you can't be fired up more than you've ever been before and reach for—and achieve—unbelievable, extraordinary, outrageous results!

Getting Fired Up! means all kinds of things to different people; in this book, I'm going to tell you what it means to me.

It's time to take a new picture of yourself. You can't look at yourself the same way anymore—I won't let you! And don't you dare think Fire Up! is just some rah-rah fluff. The Fire Up! I'm talking about is the slow and steady fire that burns forever. It's the fire within you that fuels your passions. When you truly Fire Up!, the people around you either melt or ignite!

And remember one thing—what you give, you get to keep. When you Fire Up!, you'll give some of your fire to everyone you know and everyone you meet—and they'll give it back to you, increased 10,000-fold—I promise!

Now, you may have read my book, <u>MLM Nuts $ Bolts</u>. You may have listened to my tapes, and you may have even been to one of my seminars. But even if you have, pretend that this is the first time we have been together.

In order for you to learn anything, first you've got to want to be taught. Why? Because the mind is like a parachute: It won't work unless it's open!

Begin saying things like, "I'm a good coach . . . I can really do it for me . . . I'm going to help me . . ."

Will these ideas work for you? I honestly don't know. The best way to learn is to be wide open, try new ideas on for size, and if they fit—wear them. If you can't use what you learn here, if they don't fit, throw them out and take back what you knew before. No harsh feelings and no harm done.

We're more alike than we are different, you and I—and in this book there are ideas that will help you build a ten million dollar annual sales organization.

The quality of your life is the quality of your communication.

Begin to live the philosophy of "CANI"— Constant and Never-Ending Improvement.

Enjoy hearing other points of view, but really only learn from those who have been out there doing it.

I am a voracious reader and I love movies. If you can get just one idea out of a book or from a movie, or out of a song, it's wonderful and exciting to add that idea to your life.

What determines your happiness?

Is it the weather, your income, the government, politics, the fact that someone loves you or not, your relationships, your mother, your father, the economy, your neighbors? What really determines your happiness?

Every day people use all kinds of excuses as to why their sales are not good or why their recruiting is not up, or their sponsoring is not as successful as they want. That's one of the things I've found doesn't work for me. I will not play the game of excuses.

There are excuses why you do not get things accomplished, and there are reasons why you do. Nothing in life has any meaning except for the meaning that you give it. We are in charge of our time here on Earth and it's not what has happened to you in the past that makes the real difference—it's what you're going to do right now from today on.

That makes the difference.

You can't change what happened five minutes ago. You can only take today and start building on a brighter and better and bigger tomorrow.

Here is the Ultimate Success Formula:

Know your outcome!

What is it you're trying to accomplish?

Most people know what they *don't* want, and that's what they focus on. The challenge is, if you focus on what you don't want, that's often *precisely* what you get! Begin focusing on what you DO want.

Life seems to test us, and here's an "F" word that will give you an A+ on all of life's tests: The word is *Faith*. Master yourself. Be faithful to what you're going to do, and master yourself so that you get better and better and better every day. Improve yourself every single day.

Get better. Get better. Get better.

Not a lot. Just a little.

There are people who earn $25,000 a year—and people doing the very same thing in the very same place at the very same time who are earning $250,000. What's the difference?

Is the high income earner who's making 10 times more money really 10 times better? 10 times smarter? 10 times more passionate . . . more talented . . . more motivated . . . ?

No way!

All you have to do to get better a tiny little bit each day. That's all it takes.

If you can get just one third of one percent better every day, in one year, you'll be 100 percent better than you were when you started. Think of it—100 percent better! That's *twice as good* as you are now.

Think about it.

Quit dabbling. You'll never get to your goal if you are a dabbler. You will never accomplish anything if you are a dabbler—and most people are dabblers.

People say, "Maybe I'll do it in six months . . ." That is called a "death rattle."

Another phrase that people say is, "I'll try." That's a death rattle, too.

You have to get a sense of urgency about your life and work. Remember what Yoda said in the Star Wars movie? "Luke, you either do, or do not—there is no try."

The people who win do not try. The people who win just do it. They *Fire Up!* and Just Do It!

You cannot compete with anyone else—you just compete with yourself.

Don't make the mistake of comparing yourself with anybody else. That's a dead-end game. The only one to compare yourself to is you.

You know why? Because there's not another one like you. You are unique.

A better and better you. A constantly and never-ending improvement of you. That's the goal.

And guess what:
Have the greatest poems already been written?
Have the greatest masterpieces been painted?
Has the greatest music been written and composed?
The greatest newsletters been published?
The greatest successlines been built?

NO WAY!

You've got to change and change and change and change again. You don't have a choice. Everything's always changing anyway, and if you don't change too, you'll be left behind. Take for example the automobile industry. Wouldn't it be sad if the car manufacturers said, "No more new cars, ladies and gentlemen, for the next five years." People want new automobiles—they want what is newest and latest and best, and isn't it fun to see the new shapes and colors out on the expressway?

What if the computer industry said, "That's it, folks. We've gone as far as we can. We are not going to introduce anything new. We're not going to change anything. We're just going to keep everything as it is right now."

It wouldn't work. People want the newest, what's

better and best—something to help make life faster, easier, safer, richer, more productive.

Another example is the old country singers versus the new country singers. The old country singers gave us wonderful memories we enjoyed so much. Listen to the new country singers and all the entertainment they are giving us. Listen to the difference in their style of singing, to what they are singing about. It is so much fun to see what is going on.

New is better. Change is best.

Be prepared to change. People who can change, people who will give new leadership to their groups in Network Marketing, are the ones who are going to see the greatest growth in this industry as we move into the next century.

Modeling the actions of those men and women who are already living the results in the direction that you are going is a real key. These people point you in the right direction—a direction where you're going to stay *Fired Up!*

Your selection of the little words you choose to say controls your destiny. Here are some words that you must take out of your vocabulary.

Write them down. Grab a pen. Make some notes:
Failure
Mistake
Wrong
Lying
Frustrated
Worried
Problem
Fear . . .

F-E-A-R is a big word. It looks little, but it's big; it stands for **"False Evidence Appearing Real."**

Are there any more words you can add to your list of words to get rid of?

Take an experience you had and look at what you did or did not learn from it, or achieve from it. Masters always look at their experiences and they grow from them.

I do not believe in failure.

When you've had a challenge just say,

"You know, I just learned something."

You start winning the moment you choose to grow. You start being a leader when you act out your growth. Develop yourself to become a leader.

Be an example. Be inspiring. Be response-able.

Here are some How-to *Fire Up!* strategies you can use:

1. Get yourself to consistently produce a positive result.
2. Help someone else to get a consistent, positive result.
3. Lead someone somewhere positive.

You have to get the right strategies; otherwise you're putting a lot of energy into a direction where it won't do any good. It's like running east looking for the sunset. That doesn't work. Get a new strategy.

It's just like having a brand new computer. When you first get a new computer, sometimes it's challenging. You try the old applications you used to know how to do and they don't work anymore. But once you master the new programs you can work on the different applications and it becomes a lot of fun . . . and such a time saver . . . and the power of the new computer really opens up new possibilities for you.

Stretch yourself and know that might be a challenge for a little while. But after you use new ideas over and over again, they will become fun—and so very, very productive.

Have you heard people say, "It's lonely at the top?" Well, here's some news . . . It's not lonely at the top— just very, very productive. Actually, there's nothing like the view from the top!

Make a commitment to yourself to do something

which seems beyond your present ability or skill. And make a public commitment to those who will hold you to it.

Acquire the physiology—get your whole body into it—of being totally unstoppable. Put on an "I must" attitude and begin to learn more quickly. Our world is changing so rapidly, we have got to be ready to change. What took generations to change, what used to take 50 years to change, is now changing in only five years or less.

You have to get new skills and learn new and better ways of doing your business.

Learn how to learn. That's the best thing to do.

How?

Borrow someone else's winning strategies.

There's no shame in borrowing. Who said you have to make up everything brand new all by yourself? Borrow away. Look over the other person's shoulder and copy down the answers—that is, if the person is successful. Use everything that works and throw away what doesn't work.

I've been learning strategies from others all my life and that is the key to my success.

If you're ready to grow and to get bigger and better and brighter and more excited, more *Fired Up!*, then say "YES."

Here is a great quote by Dag Hammersköld:

To all that has been, I say, "Thanks."
To all that will be, I say, "Yes."

Begin to listen, to grow, to learn, to change and

become a top communicator. Study the top communicators. Study the people who say, "Yes."

"But if I say 'Yes,' I could mess up . . . I could get hurt." True, you could. You will. You know we all experience pain. We have to expect it. We have to permit it. Pain is a signal. Pain is saying something is not working. It's just a direction sign, it points you in another, better direction.

Join a team that will challenge you, that will set you on a course that is challenging and fun.

Be respectful of others even when they're not respectful of you.

When you agree with something I say or write, that's nice—and it makes me feel good. But if you really think about it, it's the things I say that you disagree with that have the most promise of making a difference for you. It's harder to face those things. Agreement is more comfortable—and we do like our comfort zones.

From this book, or anything else in your life: Take the best and leave the rest.

And here is another "F" word for you: "Follow-through." If you're going to be successful in Network Marketing, you must follow through. Follow through with your thoughts, follow through with your deeds, follow through with your promises. And Follow-up!

Here are **"Six Simple Steps for Success:"**

1. GET INTO NETWORK MARKETING.

There will be a day when Network Marketing gets <u>into</u> you. When <u>that</u> happens, you will be the success that you can and deserve to be.

2. USE YOUR PRODUCTS.

Start using all the products that you can in your own home.

3. RECRUIT PEOPLE.

Recruiting people into your Network Marketing business is not difficult. You need only sponsor five to ten active distributors to begin reaching lasting residual income. The more people you recruit and sponsor, the higher your bonus checks will be.

4. ATTEND ALL THE BEST MEETINGS, SEMINARS AND FUNCTIONS.

Only attend those meetings and functions that are taught by people who get results and those who are constantly learning and growing. Get informed and stay in touch with what's happening with your business. Associate with other people who are of like mind and like feeling.

5. HAVE FUN.

This is mandatory! To *be* the success you deserve in Network Marketing, you need to enjoy what you're doing. Isn't it exciting to be around exciting people? You see, you do most what you like best, and you like best what you do most. Enjoy what you are doing. Have fun. It's mandatory.

6. FEED YOUR MIND.

Begin a program of personal growth and development.

Leadership

You can make our world a better place.

Each person has the chance to be a leader at some time; at home, at work, or in the community. To be a great leader is a demanding challenge. Great leaders touch people's hearts and minds. They're able to persuade others to follow them, because they have worthwhile goals that will benefit others and they have a vision of how those goals will be achieved.

A leader is an individual who knows the way, goes the way and has charisma—that special inspiring quality of leadership.

Charisma is personal confidence as opposed to job confidence—the feeling that someone really knows what they are doing. Charisma is feeling comfortable with your own greatness. It's the ability never to appear uncomfortable, simply because you are comfortable with what you're doing—that's what you are. It is really the ability to subtly cause others to respond to you, as opposed to your reacting to them.

People with charisma seem to be in charge of their lives. They seem to have a goal, a purpose, a direction.

An ounce of energy is worth a pound of technique. Charisma is pure energy—not technique.

Napoleon said that there are no bad soldiers,

only bad officers. Great generals know that you have to put your troops first. That's why they often eat in the mess hall with their troops. A team's morale often depends on small things like that.

Respect every person's dignity.

Lead by example.

There are many reasons people want to lead:

Some see a chance for power, prestige and privilege. But many—the ones who become <u>real</u> leaders—look beyond that to the greatest good of others. Service to others is what leadership is all about. Today, we call that being a Servant Leader. Do you have these qualities?

Leaders . . .

- [ ] faithfully carry out personal, family, religious and civic duties.
- [ ] seek to serve and lead others rather than to dominate them.
- [ ] show action and initiative when tempted to do nothing.
- [ ] speak up for justice, even when it is not convenient.
- [ ] encourage the downhearted.
- [ ] take unpopular but essential stands.
- [ ] forego some luxuries to help those who have little or nothing.
- [ ] respect the personality and freedom of others.
- [ ] respect and care for themselves and develop their God-given talents.

Practically everything you hear or read about leadership focuses on what "the leader" does—as though leadership were a solo performance. But when you look and study leaders out there in the real world, you find that they all have assembled teams. In MLM, call your downline your "team" or "successline."

One sure way to develop stronger leadership skills is by learning to communicate effectively. "It is not enough to know what to say, it is necessary also to know how to say it," believed the Greek philosopher Aristotle.

❑ Think before you speak.

❑ Organize your thoughts.

❑ Decide what to say and how to say it before you open your mouth.

❑ Keep the other person in mind.

❑ Try to understand another's point of view and concerns.

❑ Avoid sarcasm, personal insult or patronizing remarks.

❑ Communicate with your eyes and know that this is more than just eye contact. It's easier to know if you are making your point if you look right at your listeners.

❑ Be a good listener. Pay attention without interrupting. Learn from the ideas of others.

Leadership, at times, involves difficulties, misunderstandings, and risk. Determination and persistence are essential qualities of leadership.

Great leaders, those who accomplish the greatest good for people, know that to lead is to serve. They discover what others need and strive to help them live up to their potential. They are great servants.

And for those times when we follow rather than lead, it pays to think things through. Asking, "How does this serve?" always brings you out on the winning side of the coin toss in any situation.

☐ Know what to look for in a leader. Ultimately, you are always responsible for your own decisions, for leading your own life.

☐ If you are a leader, strive to improve.

If you want to be a leader, you can be. The choice is yours.

☐ Do not work with the people who struggle for power with you. Just let them have it.

Leaders want people on their teams who are enthusiastic, inquisitive and who thrive on change, excitement, enthusiasm, and on their work.

True leaders are totally committed to their business.

The leader who develops these skills will become important to people, and will want to work with them to develop a winning program.

If after completing a year, you can look back and have pride in the progress made by the individuals in your successline and your whole successline is collectively working to its full potential, you can easily justify all the sacrifices you have made.

Technology also plays an important role. Leaders need fax modems, cellular phones and computers in their businesses. It is imperative to make use of these tools and they will save you so much time.

And time is a leader's most precious resource.

☐ Desire to do your best, to inspire your successline and challenge them to be their best.

❏ Be capable of doing things well even though you're not a super performer. You can still be a great leader.

Some leaders do not require the same kind of personal attention that other leaders often crave.

It is okay to provide quiet, resourceful leadership.

❏ When a great leader who gets results talks, the smart leaders listen very carefully.

❏ A successful successline cuts across all social, ethnic and cultural levels, and gives everyone something to share.

❏ You have to commit yourself to become a leader. So you say, "Okay, Jan—I say "yes" to becoming my best. I am going to be the most fantastic leader in my company. I am ready to Fire Up! today."

Will you say that?

Here is a **Simple Success Philosophy** for financial prosperity:

Before financial success can occur, personal growth must occur.

So, where do you start?

❏ Well, the real question is, *why* do you want to start? Get clear on this.

❑ Define for yourself what it is you want. Is it friendship . . . financial freedom . . . fellowship . . . mission . . . what do you want? You must do this before you begin.

Then . . .

❑ You have got to get in—you have to get started.

❑ Use your own products and services.

❑ Get busy sponsoring and duplicating, attending meetings and functions, and have some fun. Make sure you use my duplicatable training system (order form in back of book).

❑ Learn your business and do your business.

Don't buy a 50-yard line seat. Don't you want to be on the playing field? Pay attention to what John Fogerty sings: "Put me in, coach. I'm ready to play. Look at me, I can be centerfield."

❑ Teach your business. Teach it to yourself through tapes and books. Teach it to others. There are all kinds of "how to" tapes and books out there.

❑ Listen to tapes all of the time.

❑ Turn your car into a classroom. You can get a Masters degree or a Ph.D. just listening to tapes in your car. I did. So can you.

❑ Make certain you get <u>MLM Nuts $ Bolts</u> manual and tapes.

Readers are leaders, and leaders are readers.

❑ Teach others to teach this business. It will help you internalize what you teach.

❑ Coach everyone, at all levels in your organization.

❑ Coach everybody who wants your leadership.

❑ Adopt this distinct philosophy: As long as someone is in your organization, they are part of your successline. All distributors, regardless of status, get the same consideration.

Those leaders who have been the most successful are usually the ones actively involved in "on the field" day-to-day leadership.

Network Marketing people will get results for a hands-on leader, because they identify with you as being an integral part of the successline.

☐ Work with your individual distributors and be actively involved in training and meetings, rather than standing remotely apart from everyone.

☐ Be proud to coach your successline.

☐ Love being part of an explosive successline. It works! It works to be excited and *Fired Up!* All the challenges and self-sacrifices of leadership will seem secondary when you're *Fired Up!*

Think clearly and become fully focused.

For things to change, you must change.

For your successline to grow, you must grow.

You can only change yourself, you cannot change other people. When a leader changes, develops and grows, so does the successline.

Ask yourself this question, "If I contin-ue to do what I have always done, I am going to continue to make what I have always made . . . and is that enough?"

You can become more effective every year . . . every month . . . even every day. You can consistently learn and earn while you learn and get better and better. Just retain your enthusiasm. Just love learning and earning.

When you start becoming more of a symbolic leader, instead of being directly involved with leading day-to-day, you'd better start looking for career alternatives—because your lack of input will begin to affect your successline negatively. This erosion may be gradual and may not be demonstrated immediately, but it will happen, believe me.

You sacrifice so much in time and energy as a leader, that as the years wear on, you will wonder, as I have wondered, "How can I still sustain my efforts?"

You have to. Find a way. Find your way.

☐ Demonstrate complete composure and control to your successline, even in impossible situations.

☐ Be forgiving. Sometimes people just don't forgive each other. Some people just want to punish others—to get back at them. Have you ever done that? Please don't do it anymore. Forgive people who hurt you and move on.

☐ Set your dreams high. Successful leaders set their dreams high. Don't allow anyone to lower your dreams for you. They can't do that without your consent. No matter what else is true in this life, *you* are in complete control of your dreams. They belong to no one else. No one else has any business with your dreams without your permission.

What is your fondest expectation?
What is out of the realm of real for you?

KNOW THIS: *If you can dream it, you can achieve it! Your dreams are going to see you through.*

Preparation, will always distinguish fine leadership. Network Marketing is a business—and you have to treat it like a business.

❏ Develop the characteristics, goals and skills you need to be a successful business person.

❏ Learn all about your company.

❏ Learn from all of your experiences—from victories as well as defeats. Leverage your learning by learning from the victories and defeats of others, too.

Your attitude is so important to your business; you can't succeed with a temperamental personality that's constantly and unpredictably going up and down. Get that under control. Constant mood swings drive your teammates and your upline and successlines crazy. You're the leader. Be stable. In the company of your successline, get it together and keep it that way.

❏ Replace negatives with positives.

❏ Learn great habits.

❏ Practice the successful methods over and over

again.

"PDR"—*Practice, Drill and Rehearse.*

❏ Grow your own leaders. Make them fabulous leaders.

❏ Don't spend much time with those people who aren't doing anything There are different levels of your leadership commitment and it's important to know what they are.

There are some so-called leaders who say they're going to "give it a try." You can't say that.

Some say, "I'll do my best."

Instead, you say, "I am really committed. I am giving it my best, and I am going to give it my best for as long as it takes to get the job done."

Ask yourself: What happens in six months if it doesn't work out? Am I going to quit? What about the six months after that?

❏ Don't quit. You must not quit. You must never give up. It is always too soon to quit. The sad part about so many people in this business is they quit before payday.

❏ Have stickability.

❏ Do not promise what you can't deliver. You have to say and have the attitude, "I'm going to do whatever it takes to get the job done."

❏ Work with your top sellers and top recruiters.

❏ Develop more top sellers and top recruiters. That's how to get the job done.

❏ Help others get what they want and realize that, just like waves, people come and go. For security in Network Marketing, the only answer is—have long term committed leaders.

❏ Only measure your organization by the number of

leaders, not in numbers of distributors or wholesale consumers or retail customers.

Professionals in this business build leaders: they make them strong and help them become successful.

❑ Develop one leader a month.

❑ Keep developing leaders.

Leaders know how to change how they think—it's a skill, a technique. That's all. And you can learn any skill.

Have you asked yourself, "Why be a leader?"

"Well, why not?"

"And why not you?"

"And why not now . . . ?"

Why not be the top performing leader in your company?

Why not double your sales targets this year—and achieve them?

Why not double your recruit targets this year—and reach them, too?

Why not do it all?

Life is too risky just to take a casual glance at the fundamentals of personal development, of goal setting, of time management and many other subjects so necessary for your team success and leadership. Absorb these ideas! Make them yours.

❑ Never let it be said that you were found **not trying**

or not searching or not dreaming of a better life. Keep looking for the few things that make the most difference.

❑ The best kept secret of the rich is time management.

❑ Make an urgent effort now—make things happen right now.

How many hours a day do the rich have? Twenty-four hours, right? And how many hours a day do you have? Same number—twenty-four hours a day.

You have to spend major time on major things.

Spend minor time on minor things.

It's the set of the sail, not the wind, that determines your course of action.

Do you know this wonderful poem by Emma Wheeler Wilcox? It's one of my favorites. Here, read this . . .

One ship drives east another drives west
With the selfsame winds that blow.
'Tis the set of the sails
And not the gales
Which tells us the way to go.
Like the winds of the sea are the winds of fate,
As we voyage along through life,
'Tis the set of the soul
That decides its goal
And not the calm or the strife.

❑ Don't ask for a better wind, ask for better poems, better books and tapes. Devour them. Set your sails. Do not let any one person or any single event or bunch of events blow you off course! You choose the set of your own sails. No one else has the power to do that.

> "*No one can make you feel inferior without your consent.*"

> —Eleanor Roosevelt

I chose to set my sails after my mentor, Jim Rohn, said, "If you will change, Jan, everything in the world will change for you."

☐ Do not wish it were easier—wish to be stronger.

There are no weaknesses—only strengths you have yet to develop.

☐ Wish for challenges and embrace them when they come. With challenges come personal growth.

☐ Wish for the right books, the right tapes, the right person to help you along, the right information.

One way to learn to do a lot of things right is . . . do a lot of things wrong.

If it takes six to ten years to prove your point, that's too long.

Do you want to continue like you are living now?

Do you want to persist in working the way you are working now?

Do you want to keep leading the way you're leading now?

☐ Benefit from your experiences, and even better, OPE—Other People's Experiences.

☐ Learn from your failures—it's too bad that the people who fail don't give seminars on how to avoid their experiences.

☐ Learn from negatives. That's what they're for.

☐ Find what the poor people read—*and do not read it.*
☐ Find out where they go—*and do not go there.*
☐ Listen to their vocabulary—*and do not use their words.*
☐ Learn from success, as well. Observe everything that's going on. Life is your classroom.

There are two important words for the end of the 90's and the 21st century, and I've taught these to my successline. The words are: *"Pay attention!"*

Someone is out there doing it right. Stop. Look. Listen.

I keep telling you, read all the books.

Learning is the beginning of wealth and health. Look at a successful person's library. What do you think it says? It screams, "Here is a library of a serious student!"

Why?

Leaders are students. That's what makes them such superb teachers—and every leader is a teacher.
☐ Don't be lazy in your learning.

You cannot invest money in any better way than on your own personal and professional education. Your personal growth, your personal development, is the most undervalued stock on the market. If you do not change, if you do not make *you* worth more—every day—it's your own fault.
☐ Please, find teachers willing to teach you. Look for them. Seek them out.

The first six years in this business, I really messed up. The second six years of my career, book by book, seminar by seminar, practice by practice, I did it and did it BIG.

Increasing your knowledge is the key.

What is easy to do is also easy not to do.

❑ Sort through this information, make a decision, try something that makes sense, ponder it.

❑ Don't neglect to do the easy things, the little things, the simple day-in day-out habits that make all the difference in your success.

❑ Pick up a book, begin to read today. Just 10 minutes. That's all you have to do—10 minutes a day.

And when you do, imagine this: Where will you be in one year? That's 3,650 minutes of learning . . . 60-plus hours—seven solid days! There are high-level, professional, week-long courses that cost $15,000 and $35,000. You can have the benefits of one in just 10 minutes a day.

Change what you're reading. That's all.

10 minutes a day. That's all.

Simple disciplines that you practice every day will make you successful.

❑ Walk away from the 97 percent of people who refuse to learn, who will not go to personal growth development seminars. Join the 3 percent—the leaders!

❑ Take charge of you. Become self-educated.

If you search . . . you will find. But in order to find, *you must search.*

❑ Never quit taking good notes and writing them in your journal. Do not miss one single idea. Taking the chance of missing something important would not be my choice. Would it be yours?

Your dreams will come true—IF you pay attention.

❑ Write down everything that the pros teach you—everything! Why? Because life changes with education.

Not only with inspiration and motivation, but with education, too.

☐ Do not let the past beat you, either. It's just water under the bridge.

☐ Do not let your past failures beat you. Just water under the bridge.

☐ Do not let your mistakes beat you. They're just water . . .

The past can be a tough school—but you have to learn from it. You cannot change what happened five minutes ago. But you can change what it did to you—how you think and feel about it *now*.

There is a price to pay to be a fine leader. Every promise has a price, and the price is easy if the promise is clear.

You can face this year—and next year, too—with apprehension if you choose, or with anticipation. You can face next year or this year, or next week, or tomorrow, with your fingers crossed.

Is that what you want?

You can't succeed all by yourself in Network Marketing. We need each other. One person does not make a symphony, but one of the things that I learned is that a symphony conductor sometimes has to turn his back on the audience.

You are so valuable, you are so important to your successline.

☐ Reach out and touch books and experiences and seminars and listen to tapes.

You can change. You can change yourself 100 percent plus!

☐ If you're ready to change say, "Yes, I am ready!"

When you walk into a room I want people to say about you, "No wonder he or she's successful."

Self-worth is so very important—and it is so exhilarating to me to see someone changing for the better.

❏ Wake up every morning and say:

"I feel happy, I feel healthy, I feel terrific. Today is going to be a great day!"

I say that every single day. Try it.

❏ All you need to be a success is a lot of people each doing a little bit. It's what Network Marketing is all about.

Here is a Formula For Disaster:
- "I should have done it,"
- "I could have done it and I didn't do it,"
- "I should have done it, I could have done it, but I will not do it."

Some people choose to live in the shadows, while others live life in the sunshine.

❏ Instead of "shoulding" all over yourself, or "coulding" on yourself, get out there and get busy.

God says, "If you plant the seed, I will grow the tree. I will bring the rain. I will bring the soil, I will bring the sun—all I need is someone to plant. That is all I need."

And isn't it great that we don't have to be the ones to make the tree? All we have to do is just plant the seeds.

❑ *Tell everybody—plant the seeds in everybody, "I am building a Network Marketing business and I need your help. Who do you know and where do they live, and will you pass on my card, and tell everybody what I'm doing."*

❑ Develop your skills. Skills will make you more valuable. They will make a fortune for you and that will make a fortune for you.

Personal development is so important.

❑ Get a better vocabulary.

❑ Get more stories to illustrate what you are saying.

❑ Develop your skills.

❑ Productivity is also another of the game's names— and remember that activity leads to productivity and success breeds success. Get more productive.

❑ Fire Up!

You're going to make measurable progress in a reasonable time. You have to be reasonable with time.

Five minutes is too short.

Five years is too long.

- In the last six years, how much money have you saved?
- In the last six months, how many classes or seminars have you taken to develop your new skills or polish up your present skills?
- In the last ninety days, how many books have you read?

❑ Set some timely goals—better sooner than later.

Success is a numbers game in Network Marketing. In order to succeed, you have to change, grow, become better, wiser, more capable than you are now.

Whatever information you do not use—you lose.

❑ Study wealth if you want to be wealthy.

❑ Stay positive. So much of this world is negative. But when you come to my meetings I want to be able to count on you to stay positive. I do not want you to gossip. I do not want to hear the bad news, I want to hear, "What can we do to change, grow, prosper and be better people?"

❑ Set personal goals.

What you really want in your business is to feel challenged during your career.

❑ Choose not to participate in recession thinking, but instead in having increased confidence.

Masters will teach you what to say and how to say it, and when you find out those secrets, you will find more business.

❑ Don't waste time on uncommitted people—do not work with the uncommitted.

Where do successful sales people come from?

They come from everywhere.

The skills you need to succeed require that you change, and you must get your silly pride out of the way to do that.

The majority of Networking companies spend hours training on business logic and product knowledge. But here is what will make a difference for you: People skills. Emotion, enthusiasm and getting *Fired Up!* This is what closes the sales.

Products do not destroy companies. People do. Most Network successlines that fold are destroyed by old leadership unwilling to change.

☐ You have to train, tolerate or terminate.

☐ Hear it, see it, write it, drive it deeper and deeper into your subconscious.

☐ Sometimes you have to experience a little pain in order to grow. But grow up, take responsibility, show maturity, apply yourself, become a complete leader.

Once people become established leaders they think they've earned the right to put forth less effort. That's not true. That's when you have to put forth even more effort.

So much of leadership is confidence. When your confidence level is up, you can take on the world. You will love it when you are the leader and everybody looks to you to do something. Don't feel pressure. Feel energized.

Here are three key words: relaxation, confidence, concentration. Each time you feel yourself losing any of them, just mention the word itself and you might just feel very different.

Your successline depends on you. You have to deliver.

Have you ever been on a road trip and you are driving and have a map but still get lost? Have you ever pulled into a filling station and asked an attendant for guidance? Someone you don't even know? A stranger? And you have trusted their directions to get you to your destination? Well, that's all *Fire Up!* is about, just look at me as your friendly filling station person who is simply giving you directions to keep you going in the direction of your destination. *Fire Up!* You are going to make remarkable progress in a short time!

You will not believe what will happen if you start recruiting, sponsoring, developing your skills and getting *Fired Up!*

Stay *Fired Up!* Just stick with it, and never give up!

Fire Up! Just do it!

Dream big! Your dreams are going to see you through!

Promoting Leaders

IN NETWORK MARKETING look for these characteristics in your successlines, pay attention, they are your leaders:

❑ AWARENESS

Be aware of all you hear and all you say. Do not repeat negative or suspect information that comes from the grapevine or the company or your upline or successline—or anyone else! A leader is a person who accurately reads all the signals from the top and the bottom of the organization. A leader understands the information honestly and clearly and gives it a common meaning for everyone.

❑ ACTION

Leaders are judged on how they act and how fast they act. Here are some questions your successline will be looking for answers to in your actions:

Does the leader avoid confrontation?

Does the leader reward results?

Does the leader ignore betrayal?

How long does it take the leader to face tough challenges?

Does the leader give due credit for victories?

☐ VISION
A great leader has the ability to visualize the future and to communicate that vision powerfully to the successline. This kind of foresight guides the successline in their actions and the actions of their followers.

☐ SELF-LEADERSHIP
A great leader has to manage self, family, and career. When you are a leader, you have to be in command of yourself and exercise your talents to meet the challenges you face. Self-leadership is a first-step requirement for leading others.

☐ RESPONSIBILITY
Average leaders expect responsibility; great leaders teach their followers how to act responsibly. The very best leaders become role models and assume responsibility for their followers' shortcomings. They are responsible for empowering the successline.

☐ RESPECT
Leaders sell a product called leadership. Followers buy it. Leaders respect their followers and treat them as their valued customers.

☐ SELF-IMPROVEMENT
Lead by example. When you are not improving yourself, it is hard to urge others to do so. The leader is as the leader does.

☐ BE SERVICE ORIENTED
Leaders understand that no matter what you do for

a living, you are in a service business. You must first ask yourself what others need, not what you need: "How will this serve?"

☐ **ENERGY**
Leaders radiate positive energy and sidestep negative energy. They are healthy, vital and alive. They know they need to be *Fired Up!*—and they are!

☐ **BELIEVE IN OTHERS**
Leaders affirm, see the worth, goodness and potential in others. They are champions with a cause—a cause their followers think is them.

☐ **BALANCE**
Leaders work on balancing their work, home and community in their lives—and especially balancing their business and family life. Balance is one of the most important things leaders have to teach their people.

☐ **VALUE DIFFERENCES**
See new alternatives as exciting, not threatening. If you have tried an old way of doing business, and got little or no results, that a new and different approach is the better way. If someone is getting results, *pay attention* to whatever he or she is doing.

☐ **TAKE CARE OF YOURSELF**
Leaders stay healthy physically, through exercise; mentally, through reading, listening to tapes, and attending seminars; and spiritually, through prayer or inspiration. You will rarely hear a leader complain.

Building leaders who are building leaders is the only way to have a huge organization.

And if that is your goal then here are some tips:

☐ Find the people in your group or successline that turn in sales—no matter how much—consistently.

☐ Support them with recognition in monthly newsletters and encourage them to recruit and build a business.

☐ Remember, not everyone wants your leadership. There are complainers and whiners that actually expect you to do it for them.

☐ Look for the sellers who least expect your help.

☐ Send out a "Future Manager (or Executive, or whatever your first real leadership position is) Newsletter" to all those in your successline who have the potential to become leaders, or have a "1-800" number for people to call in to get a phone blast message, or create a website loop.

☐ Every time you get a new recruit's paperwork in your office, the very first thing to do is send them a "Welcome to our successline" letter and a complimentary copy of your newsletter. Go to *www.fireup.com* to get free ideas from *The Network Flame* monthly newsletter.

☐ Always return phone calls within 24 hours, so people know that you are dependable.

Once people see they can become a team leader, they realize they can keep going on up the ranks. They just needed help getting those first few recruits.

There are times that you might not wish to promote new leaders, but want to strengthen your existing leaders.

☐ Don't promote weak leaders—those with only five or six people in their organizations. Promote people who have ten or more people in their organization who are intent on business-building. You need a lot of people each doing a little bit to gain the momentum for building a big organization.

☐ Have contests!

You can whip a horse and it will not move, but put a carrot in front of its nose and it will follow you anywhere! Forget whips in this business. Use carrots.

Trying to get your sales people to turn in big sales is nowhere near as productive as getting a lot of people turning in something small—consistently, each and every month.

☐ Set the expectation in your newsletter that some people will be promoted. If someone has the desire they will normally give you signals—like calling you before you call them.

Fire Up! Just do it!

Criticism

Let Criticism Motivate You.

Take it upon yourself as a personal challenge for your team to have the greatest year ever. You can accomplish your goals and ignore the critics.

Here's a formula for re-establishing communication after being personally criticized:

Find a way—any way—to acknowledge something the other person has done, whether it's a project they've done or good decision they've made, outside of the original dispute. Don't expect to resolve all your philosophical differences with just one conversation. You'll have to work at it over time. Be sensitive to each person's personality and find a way to account for it in your day-to-day work. It's important to keep lines of communication open and remind yourself of your respect for others.

The point is not whether you are right or wrong. Even if you feel you're right and the other person is wrong, you have to make the effort to resume communication. You can't afford to let the dispute fester, because the longer you wait the more entrenched it becomes.

☐ Do not let criticism dominate your thoughts.

☐ Be involved in the challenge of keeping your successline moving forward.

The life of a true leader is so intense it does not make sense to give much thought to your reputation, or to what people are saying. Being a leader is a high-profile job.

❑ Have a strong drive to meet your career goals. Your drive will sustain you through the challenging years. Just say "Oh, well," and move on. Simply move on.

❑ Realize that some people need to have a negative subject to dwell on, and that it's much easier to take a critical view of someone from a distance.

❑ Do not deflect responsibility. So many ideas and suggestions come out of a successline that no one can be concerned about whose creation it was.

❑ Be cautious of false relationships. When you feel that a friendship has turned cold, remind yourself that it most likely was not a friendship in the first place. Real friends do not criticize one another

❑ Realize that people just telling you they're the sharing and caring kind can sometimes mean they are caring and sharing only if you share and care about them, according to *their* rules.

There are no statues erected in the world to critics.

Critics free you from unhealthy relationships you think were important but actually do nothing to further your business or yourself.

If you can't say anything nice, don't say anything at all.

Here's a quote I cherish about criticism:

The Critic

It's not the critic who counts—not the man who points out how the strong man stumbled, or where the doer could have done better. The credit belongs to the man who is actually in the arena, whose face is marred by dust and sweat and blood. Who strives valiantly, who errs and comes up short again and again, who knows the great enthusiasms, the great devotions, and spends himself in a worthy cause . . . Who, at the least knows, in the end, the triumph of high achievement, and who, at the worst, if he fails, at least fails while doing greatly, so that his place shall never be with those cold and timid souls who know neither victory or defeat.

—Theodore Roosevelt

When you're the leader, you're going to face naturally resulting criticisms and gossip.

Critics . . . lead, follow, or get out of the way!

Ask yourself: Why do I want to have a relationship with someone who is not supportive of me, or my methods?

Attention unsupportive spouses who are unable to support their spouses building a Network Marketing business: you are very short-sighted. I feel quite sad for you.

Many times, it's just that they only see the dollars going out. Yet, if they would have patience, their spouses would quite possibly make more money than they ever dreamed.

If you hear of some of your successline's spouses say that <u>you</u> are one of the only ones making a lot of money in <u>your</u> company, encourage them . . . if they would only be supportive so their spouses could be more free to recruit, teach and train others to be successful, their spouses would make more money—faster.

Normally, someone who responds this way is just an insecure spouse.

However, if the Networking person is not working and is unwilling to do whatever it takes to change and get results, then I am supportive of the spouse who is frustrated!

Results speak loud and clear.

Excuses speak loud and clear, too.

There are reasons why people are successful and excuses why they are not.

When you build a Network Marketing Organization to over 7,000 plus people, train over 20,000 people, and earn over $300,000 a year, write two books, and produce music and audio cassettes, all while raising three children . . . I will buy your material!

But I won't buy your excuses—ever!

❑ Learn to thrive on chaos!

❑ Be different.

Who wants to be average? If you're average you are the best of the worst and the worst of the best. Think on that for a minute . . . *Don't be average!*

Collectively, in any organization a mentality develops—it's almost a herd instinct. When a topic is hot, and it's often initiated by some prominent or controversial person, virtually everyone chases it, each person looking for a different angle or insight.

As years pass, you will find that trying to keep everyone happy in your company will make you exhausted.

❏ Relax, reflect, and take pride in your success.

Adversity does build character.

❏ Each time you get criticized, analyze yourself to see what went wrong and then work on improving your skills.

When faced with a challenge you have two choices:

1. Quit and walk away.
2. Stay and meet the challenge head on.

❏ Don't stay down. Winners are seldom discouraged—at least not for long.

❏ Never give up, your dreams are going to see you through, I promise.

You might get down occasionally, burned out, but do not let it control you or your results.

❏ Analyze the challenge, learn from it, and then get on with the business of winning.

Here's a quote from the Native Americans:

"Iroquois chiefs are expected to possess an ability to handle criticism with 'a skin seven times thick,' and they're expected to control their own and others' negative thoughts and feelings, as well. These leaders are also required to consider the effects of their policies, down to the seventh generation."

What do you expect of yourself . . . ?

Critics are everywhere—just keep helping those who want your leadership and let go of those who do not. Letting go of critics gives them nothing to hold on to and they disappear sooner or later.

You will still prosper and grow without the critics. It's okay. They're not required.

You're okay. Just get *Fired Up!*

You'll be fine.

Never give up—your dreams are going to see you through.

Ignite your passion and Fire Up!

"People do that which they want to do."
—Edith Knowles

How to Just Do It!

HAVE YOU HEARD OF THE "survival bubble?"

Most people go to the edge of the boundary of where they think they can go—and then stop. Yet, all of the greatest accomplishments in life and work have been achieved beyond that stopping point—outside of the survival bubble. Whose air do we breathe? It is not my air, or your air. It's free for all of us all over the world.

Your car, the building you are in, the park you're sitting in, are filled with radio waves. Are they yours, mine? I don't think so—They're free, they're everyone's.

The world is full of information. Whatever you need to know already exists somewhere like air and radio waves. It's available to all of us. You might have to go to someone's library to get the information that will help you build your Network Marketing organization, but it's all there already.

❑ Associate with like-minded people. They're out there, too, just like radio towers.

❑ You have to want to do this and you have to want it very badly. You've got to move outside of your survival bubble.

❑ If you are not capable of receiving, you are not capable of giving.

❑ Live beyond motivation.

❑ Live your life as an *inspiration*.

The universe constantly rearranges itself to accommodate your desires. Your purpose in life will be right if it is simple and you feel it deeply—and that means if it inspires you. It's a picture the universe can follow.

❑ Find out what your purpose is as a leader. Movement will begin when you do.

People want to be around someone who knows where they're going. If you have clear-cut goals, you will have a wonderful time in your life and work.

❑ Focus on what you want. You can produce outrageous and outstanding results.

❑ Focus your attention, determine what <u>you</u> want to accomplish.

Results on results . . .

Success on success . . .

Most people focus on what they don't want.

Focus on what you don't want and I promise you are going to get it. Focus on what you do want and the same holds true.

It's the focus that matters, not the wanting or not wanting—because whatever you focus on is what you'll get. That's the power of your attention. That's why we say, "Pay attention." And what you pay for is the result of where you're focusing.

Here are two powerful words to always remember:

"I AM."

❑ Be very careful about what follows these words when you speak—even if only when speaking to yourself.

When you say, "I am tired . . . I am mad . . . I am insulted . . ."—it's disempowering!

Most people focus on the resentment from the past. Live *NOW*. The past is gone. Bye!

❑ Experience a gratitude attitude. Repeat it to yourself over and over and over until it becomes part of you:

To all that has been—Thanks!

To all that will be—Yes!

Life is so short . . . too short.

❑ Choose your own reality. CPA: *Create, Promote and Allow.*

❑ Be accountable for your life. PMA: (Positive Mental Attitude) also means *Productive, Meaningful Action.* Your actions—and only your actions—are what produce results for you. Learn while you earn.

❑ Provide more value than people expect.

❑ Put people first, and success will follow.

❑ The most common way of inspiring people is through your own personal example.

❑ Set an example.

❑ If you want your successline to sell, then you had better be selling.

❑ If you want your group to recruit, then you had better be recruiting.

❑ Set successline goals.

❑ Set annual goals.

❑ Set your own personal goals.

❑ Set daily goals.

❑ Set weekly goals.

❑ If you want your successline to set goals, then you must be setting goals.

❑ Everything you want from your successline, you must first do yourself.

❑ Stay ahead of your successline if you want to keep leading them.

❑ Put a lot of thought into your business.

❑ Pass on everything good that you learn—do not hold back.

Remember King Midas?

Remember the Bible: "Give and ye shall receive."

Who is the better teacher: Midas or Jesus?

❑ Answer your phone.

❑ Tell people that you are in this business for a life-time.

❑ Tell them about your regular meeting schedule and your travel plans.

❑ Offer such an abundance of support that they will know beyond a shadow of a doubt that success is inevitable on your team.

❑ Don't fear success.

Most people are afraid of not succeeding. They are literally scared to death of failure. This single fear is the biggest obstacle in getting them on the road to success.

❑ The ambitious people are easy to identify. They are a joy to work with.

❑ Work closest with the people who are willing to cooperate with your methods and who are coachable and teachable.

It's not the smartest people who succeed today. It's the ones who are most open. Ambitious people are the most open. They are the most willing to change. And in our ever-faster-changing world, who is more likely to succeed than people who are open and willing to change?

❑ If you do not have enough ambitious people in your successline, then concentrate on recruiting more.

❑ Stop trying to squeeze business out of reluctant people!

❑ Tell them how to do your business.

❑ Show them how, and be patient with them.

❑ Give meetings at homes of the ambitious people under them.

❑ Do not waste time trying to prove your point and convince others. This is not the *convincing* business. It's a *sorting* business—you sort through people to find the ambitious ones, the ones who are ready, willing and able.

It's a waste of your time (and theirs) to try to force someone beyond the rank of the beginning entry level of Network Marketing if that is all they want from your company.

Water seeks its own level. So do people.

❑ Teach others so they can teach others to reach others.

❑ Always reach up for the next rung on the ladder of your success, otherwise you are never going to get to the top. And once you get to the next rung, once you know how to do that—teach others to do what you have just done.

❑ Teach others to do what you already know how to do.

Do you know how to buy the products?

Good, teach others to do what you already know how to do.

Do you know how to bring someone into the business?

Good, teach your people how to do that, too.

Do you know how to lead a group of two, or three, or four people?

Great, teach others how to do that and you will soon be leading a group of 20 or 30, or more.

Do you see how it goes?

Do you see how your successline will build?

In some companies, the goal is to have at least four or five strong, level, committed team leaders. How many will it take in your company—do you know?

❑ Develop your depth and you develop your strength.

❑ If you always have these key first lines you are working with and qualifying, you will be very busy, happy and very prosperous.

❑ The goal is to build an organization wide and deep.

❑ Sponsor 12 people in a six-week program. Then,

by working on depth, these 12 people quickly grow to 60 people.

☐ Continue to sponsor successful representatives on a replacement basis with total team volume as your goal. Remember, this is a business. Do this and you will be the leader of a nationwide Network and, once it's established, it's like a train that has left the station. It's unstoppable!

☐ Copy things that *work* for others. Your business will grow much faster when others can see and feel all the fun you're having. You'll also work harder when you're having fun—and isn't that nice!

☐ Develop, understand, and maintain the attitude and desire to build an organization that you can manage and lead. You don't have to buy it. In fact, you can't buy it.

☐ If you want more, produce more.

☐ Concentrate on doing what is right rather than doing things right.

☐ Get in, get done, and get out and get on with it. Work fast.

☐ Concentrate on what you do best, and let others do the rest.

☐ Your objective must be to get results.

☐ Ask yourself, "Should I be working on this project at all?"

☐ MPN—<u>M</u>ost <u>P</u>roductive <u>N</u>ow." You must do the most productive thing at every given moment.

☐ Teach and command respect by your example. If your successline respects you enough to learn from you, you will increase your income—all your incomes.

❑ Play no favorites.

❑ *Keep your top performers and top producers loyal by being sensitive to their need for recognition.*

❑ Have vision. Have goals that look towards the future.
   - Do you have 5-year goals?
   - Do you have 10-year goals?
   - How about 25-year goals?

❑ Attack situations and rapidly make tough decisions. Even if it is the wrong decision, make a decision.
❑ Do not avoid making decisions.
❑ Promote risk-taking—especially your own.
❑ Be a specialist at recruiting, training, and re-training top producers.

Do you know where the action is?

ACTION is where the action is.

Know that all people are motivated differently. That's why you must constantly be a student of the skills of understanding people's personalities.

You will only be as successful as your people, and they will only be as successful as you help them to become.

❑ Radiate enthusiasm.
❑ Avoid jealousy and negative thinking.
❑ Do not ever stop sponsoring and enrolling new

people.

❏ Invest in your business—invest money into your business.

❏ Invest in yourself.

❏ Refuel daily by listening to tapes and reading great books.

❏ Know that you are going to get your feelings hurt, but the highs outweigh the lows. Disappointments can make you better or bitter.

❏ Motivation does not close sales. Skill closes sales. People skills close the most sales with people.

❏ The road to success is always under construction. Dig we must.

❏ Everyone has potential—let's not waste it. Bring it forth.

❏ Get productive.

❏ Spend 80 percent of your time on your prospects and customers.

❏ Remember, if it is going to be, it is up to whom? Right, it's up to you! **"If it is going to be, it is up to me."**

"Faith that fizzles before the finish was faulty from the first."

❏ Personally recruit 50 people—and that will make a huge difference. How many people have you recruited this year?

❏ Quit needing the approval from those in your company who aren't going to give it to you.

❏ Set your goal to be Number One in your entire company.

❏ Give out hundreds of business cards. Wherever you give out your money or credit card, a business card goes too.

❏ Set a goal to give out 100 business cards in one week.

❏ Set a team goal—1000 business cards in a month. Just get out and make it happen.

❏ Get your mind off yourself.

❏ Help one person have a better, brighter day.

❏ See yourself in the year 2008. Do you know how many years from now that is? Where are you going to be in the year 2008?

❏ Remember to take lots of pictures. Pictures are worth hundreds of thousands of words. Take lots of pictures. Then what?

❏ Make slides.

❏ Invest in a slide machine and a screen. Turn those little pictures into huge pictures on the screen. Share those slides with people you love and care about.

❏ Have slide shows at your meetings and rallies.

❏ Throw away the past, but hold on to the lessons that your past has taught you.

❏ You have to be patient with yourself if you are going to make big money.

❏ You have got to change yourself. Learn and grow.

❏ Begin today to acknowledge that you are important. You are cared for and you are loved.

❏ Begin today to be a giver not a taker. *Fire Up!*— and lighten up.

❏ Be happy for those who are succeeding.

❏ Rent videos about champions.

❏ Read about champions.

❏ Throw out the old—discard it. Bring in the new.

❏ Begin to think big, and then think bigger, and

then multiply your big thoughts by 10, and then multiply them by 100, and then by 1,000.

❑ *Fire Up!*

❑ Change your attitude.

❑ Go for greatness. Why not? And if you don't do it—who will?

How do you start? Here are just a few ideas:

❑ Wash your car.

❑ Clean up your desk.

❑ Clean out your handbag or wallet.

Your car, your desk, and your handbag are reflections of your mind.

❑ Expect excellence, not perfection, from your children.

❑ Expect excellence—and not perfection—from yourself. Perfection is God's thing. Excellence is yours.

❑ Forgive someone who has hurt you—let it go.

❑ Pick up the phone and call someone that you have hurt, and clean up the mess you left.

❑ Write a letter of apology expecting nothing in return.

❑ Make room for greatness.

❑ Cut your hair.

❑ Get a massage.

❑ Get a manicure.

❑ Get rid of all those old average clothes.

❑ Move your furniture around.

❑ Buy a new compact disc.

❑ Light a candle.

❑ Become a flower fairy. The most special gift I ever received: Someone (I still do not know who did it) organized my entire successline to send fresh flowers to my home every week of the year. I call those people the "flower fairies."

☐ Send someone a bouquet of flowers for no reason.
☐ Read a book.
☐ Go get your teeth professionally cleaned.
☐ Buy some new tennis shoes.
☐ Sail away from your safe harbor. Explore all your possibilities.
☐ Know that the Big Bad Wolf is not going to come to your door.
☐ Take a risk.
☐ Watch people take a risk.
☐ Ski down a mountain.
☐ Ride a gondola up to the top of a mountain.
☐ Thank God you are alive.
☐ Do not to take any medicine that is not truly necessary.
☐ Quit complaining!
☐ Get energized.
☐ *Fire Up!*
☐ Look for an abundance in your life. You have no limitations—only the ones you say you have.
☐ Hug five people a day, and then go hug some more.
☐ Picture all your bills paid, and guess what—you'll pay them.

The speed of the leader is the speed of the pack.

☐ Present your gifts in an unusual manner.
☐ Be unique.
☐ Be better than you were yesterday.
☐ Become a saver of time.

❑ Become a saver of money.

❑ Care about people that do not know how to return the love you want. Show them how to love you.

❑ Say goodbye to those people who cannot and will not love you.

There is love for you on this planet, in this country, in your state, in your city, in your neighborhood, and from me.

❑ Learn to say BTDT: *Been There, Done That—and I'm not going to do that again!*

❑ Learn to say BTWT: *Been There, Won That!*

❑ Begin your life today with energy! Go all out! You deserve an abundant life.

As Hank Williams Jr. sings: "We all need a little less talk and a lot more action."

❑ Live with pride, love America, think of all your liberties.

❑ Dreams move on, though, if you don't do something about them. In Network Marketing, all give some, but some give all.

❑ Be the one who gives all.

❑ Some stand tough. Some have to fall. Stand tough.

❑ Never prejudge anyone. Anybody who can fog a mirror is a prospect.

❑ Listen to my *Fire Up!* tapes and <u>MLM Nuts $ Bolts</u> tapes.

❑ Turn every minute you have into a learning minute—feed your mind, feed your mind, feed your mind!

❑ Return phone calls.

❑ Answer your correspondence.

❑ Do not complain about your own personal chal-

lenges—they will pass.
- ❏ Work smart.
- ❏ Follow up every lead.
- ❏ Help others learn to prospect by modeling what you do.

In the beginning, in Network Marketing, you do a lot that you don't get paid for. But later on, you will get paid a lot for things that you do not do.

- ❏ Take notes in a journal or on a legal pad. Capture those notes. Don't let them be on little pieces of paper all over the place.
- ❏ Get a nice pen—it says you care about yourself.
- ❏ Have patience.
- ❏ When you think about quitting, start all over again.
- ❏ Get determined.
- ❏ Get the commitment.
- ❏ Get *Fired Up!*
- ❏ You can shrink your dreams to match your income, or you can choose to expand your income to match your dreams.

Did you know that your income tends to be the average income of your 10 best friends? So, if you want more income, either get new friends whose incomes are higher, or raise the income of the friends you've got now.

- ❏ Get focused and stick with your focus.

There are two ways to make more money in Network Marketing: You can move more

products or bring more people into your organization. Do both.

☐ Be willing to pay the price at the beginning when your children are young, so that they can have a fabulous future. Just never give up!

☐ Go to seminars. Improve yourself.

☐ Only work with like-minded people. Don't let it bother you that not everybody is going to want to do business in your style. You do not need the approval of everyone in your company.

☐ When you are disappointed, learn to say what my daughter Ashley taught me to say, **"Oh well."**

☐ Read books on leadership and champions. There is a reading list in <u>MLM Nuts $ Bolts.</u>

☐ Care about your people—even when they do not care about you.

☐ Take risks. Throw out what does not work.

☐ Set a goal to sponsor more people than anybody in your successline or upline.

☐ When you are not *Fired Up!*, do whatever it takes to get *Fired Up!* Put on the high energy, *Fire Up!* music so loud it can't help but get you *Fired Up!* Put on the *Never Give Up* music.

☐ Study the masters.

☐ Set the pace.

☐ Discover who for years have been your best players and do more than your best players do.

☐ Have an uncluttered workspace.

☐ Let your spouse know that you are committed.

☐ Never give up!

❑   If what you are doing is not working, stop and ask yourself some questions:

How can I do this more easily?

How can I do this more simply?

How can I do this better?

Who could help me do this, so I do not have to continue to struggle?

How much does what I am doing matter to me?

How much does what I am doing matter to my future?

What do I need right now to achieve optimum positive results in my life and work?

❑   Work very hard in the beginning months of the year. Those who work early in the year harvest in the fall. Your objective, remember, is that harvest . . . to get results. Do what it takes. Do it now.

❑   Keep your expenses as low as possible.

❑   Invest in self-development seminars, books and tapes. Remember, it is simpler to follow a pioneer than to be a pioneer.

❑   Know that you can produce outrageous results.

❑   Spend time in quiet, relaxed contemplation.

❑   Most people focus this way: have, do, be. To have something, I have to do something in order to be somebody. Look at it in another way. To be someone, I have to do something in order to have everything.

❑   Earn while you learn and sell the benefits of your company and of being associated with you.

❑   Put other people first and your success will follow.

There is no such thing as a failure—remember,

there are only quitters. When things are down, they always come back up. Just start over.

❑ Accept responsibility and say "Yes," even when it's easier to say "No."

Your people reflect you.

❑ Spend most of your time recruiting and training. You can't coast; you have got to work at it every day.

❑ Sweat the small stuff, pay attention to detail.

❑ Never be discouraged.

❑ Gladly go to work everyday. Do not look at work as drudgery or that is what it will become.

❑ Look for the doers.

❑ Have optimistic eagerness.

❑ Get more people with desire.

❑ Write more newsletters, get more enthusiasm—and stop whining and complaining!

❑ Invest in a quality tape recorder.

❑ Begin your tape library and know that this is an investment in yourself—the best one you could make.

❑ Build your own inventory.

❑ *Photocopy your bonus check. Keep a record of every bonus check that you get and show your check to your successline with enthusiasm, even if it is small. Let them see it get bigger.*

❑ Have a power picture of who you want to become.
❑ Keep your word. Do not make up excuses—don't even borrow them.
❑ Stop talking failure.
❑ Become a great communicator. That makes things happen.
❑ Do not wait for things to happen.
❑ Have a sense of urgency about your business.
❑ Challenge yourself to have certain things done by a certain date. It's called a "By when."
❑ Teach people what to do, tell them what to do, and then do it. Do the job of the person above you and you will soon have their position. Help others to succeed and be strong.
❑ Be bold—you can do it. The more you put into your business, the more you get out of it.
❑ Continue to improve.

Remember, the way you spend your time is far more important than how you spend your money. Money mistakes can be corrected, but time spent is gone forever. Spend the rest of your life saying, "I am so glad I did this," instead of, "Oh, I wish I had done that."

❑ Read, read, read. Become a reader and a leader.
❑ Listen to motivational tapes every single day.

Fire Up!—Just do it!

How to Have Great Meetings

MEETINGS ARE IMPORTANT, AND THE RIGHT KIND of meetings are really fun and get big results for you and your successlines.

Call your meetings "Team Meetings." In your meetings, you want people to exchange information, get to know each other, and have the chance to practice, drill and rehearse.

❑ Make every meeting as upbeat as possible.

❑ Humor is important in your meetings, because you want people to able to laugh together. This greatly improves their comfort level and adds to the fun.

❑ Meetings are for the growth of your organization and for the individual team members' development.

❑ Start with holding them in your home first. As your team gets larger, you can move to a hotel, preferably on the ground floor.

Meetings need to be fun and upbeat; *Fired Up!* meetings get big results.

❑ Have up-tempo music playing at the beginning of your meetings and throughout all the breaks.

❑ Be enthusiastic at your meetings. Do you know what people need to hear? "Hey, it's great to see you . . . I'm so glad to see you here." Practice saying those words.

❑ Teach fundamentals and skills and establish a positive atmosphere and attitude.

❑ Constantly throw out what does not work. Keep the best, and leave the rest.

❑ Encourage people to become partners with you in planning and conducting your meetings. This helps them stay *Fired Up!*

❑ Have people give each other hugs at meetings.

❑ Take frequent breaks—the mind cannot absorb more than the bottom can endure—and put on the *Fire Up!* music.

❑ Participate when you go to meetings. Be involved!

Meetings are exciting, fun, and, most of all, they are very productive.

All team leaders who are anxious to build their businesses in Network Marketing attend meetings and participate by watching, listening, and being one of the presenters.

❑ Make certain that the leaders are all training in a like-minded way. That way, they're all contributing to the success of each other's successline by teaching the same duplicatable system. It has to be like-minded to be successful and duplicatable.

If you have to drive about 45 minutes to an hour to get to a meeting, don't complain about the distance. Why? Because you can expect that the meetings will be productive and fun.

❑ Stay until long after the scheduled meeting is over to capture even more nuts and bolts.

❑ Use a microphone. Use it in regular meetings and in your monthly team meeting.

❑ Attend your leaders' meetings and copy their meetings—if they are getting results. Why reinvent the

wheel?
- [ ] Volunteer to help. You will gain experience at these meetings that will be invaluable.

Your attitude at meetings can inspire everyone.
- [ ] Be enthusiastic, positive and friendly.
- [ ] Be the last one to leave the meetings.
- [ ] Use as many visual aids as possible and use examples and stories wherever possible, as well.
- [ ] Stay consistent with the time, date and place of your meetings. They will become the pillar and cornerstone of your business.
- [ ] Set your meeting calendar a year in advance. It's amazing how this will help you to stay organized and busy. Your distributors will value your time more and your meetings will be larger and more effective when you do.
- [ ] Pick a meeting date and stick with it.
- [ ] Always have your products on display.
- [ ] Do not expect big crowds right away, but when you build it, they will come.
- [ ] Use ground floor meeting rooms in convenient locations.
- [ ] Set the registration table near the door on the outside of the meeting room.
- [ ] Have name tags.
- [ ] Keep the room on the cool side. If it's too warm, people get drowsy.
- [ ] Provide ice water.
- [ ] Eliminate ashtrays and smoking from around the meeting room door and in the halls.
- [ ] Have the entrance door at the rear of the meeting room.

❏ No children. Sometimes children can be disruptive even when they don't mean to be.

❏ The meeting room should be well-lit and have some displays and photographs. Pictures are worth a thousand words.

❏ Seating should be set up and ready in advance.

❏ Have additional chairs set aside until they are needed.

❏ Set less chairs than you have confirmed people.

❏ DO NOT have more chairs than people.

❏ Smile and greet everyone, and encourage your leaders to be greeters, too.

Not every meeting will be equally successful. Learn from your challenges.

❏ Encourage people to bring guests.

❏ Conduct your monthly or weekly meetings by involving your most enthusiastic representatives.

❏ Devote time to the marketing plan, remember the importance of individual recognition.

❏ Never discuss a negative thought in a group meeting.

❏ Team up with other like-minded team leaders and go to meetings with other teams to get new approaches and new ideas. Always try to get someone as good or better than yourself involved.

Your goal is to build a big Network Marketing organization, so keep your meetings geared to that goal.

❏ *Participate in a meeting as soon as possible.*

❏ *Have your own meetings as*

soon as possible.

The more practice you get, the more your meetings will improve. If your leader lives far away from you, don't wait. Start your own meeting right away. It may not be comfortable, but it's the best way to learn.

☐ Don't expect people to attend your meetings unless you ask them.

☐ If you have low attendance and not enough growth in your business, have you asked any prospects to come to your meetings? Try it!

☐ The people who regularly attend the meetings are the ones who have an interest and are committed to building their business.

☐ Sometimes your meeting is the only time and place in that week or that month that some of your people are in a positive, fun atmosphere.

☐ Be an example for others at your meetings.

☐ Be enthusiastic, positive and attentive.

☐ Treat your leaders with respect.

☐ You might find that having small meetings, scheduled at other times which do not take away from your big monthly meetings, are also very helpful. It helps you to offer more personal on-the-job training.

☐ You might choose to form your own team meetings with your own successlines, and not work with the larger meetings.

☐ Make the dress casual and not dressy.

☐ Provide baby-sitting in an adjacent room, so that you're not disrupted by crying or happy sounds from infants and toddlers.

☐ Have testimonies from those who have experienced a change in their direction in life from attending your meetings.

☐ Bring many surprises, and have lots of give-always.
☐ Teach skills and techniques, vision and leadership.
☐ Have very special awards and tons of recognition.

☐ Start and end all of your meetings with the *Fire Up!* chant. Here's how it goes:

Fire Up! (Clap, clap)
Fire Up! (Clap, clap)
Fire Up! And Up! And Up and Up and Up!
Fire Up! (Clap, clap)
Fire Up! (Clap, clap)
Fire Up! And Up! And Up and Up and Up!

You can feel the energy charge up! every time you do this chant. It's awesome.
☐ Recognize those on your team who value your leadership.
☐ Have meetings, they work!
☐ Make sure you get my *Generic Duplicatable Training System!*
Fire Up!—Just do it!

How to Recruit

RECRUITING IS SO MUCH FUN. Learn to love recruiting, sponsoring and enrolling people in Network Marketing. Why? It IS just *so much fun!* It's the key to building your business.

Go for the numbers.

If somebody says "No" to you, just go out your front door and scream, "Next!" There will be somebody next. Someone is just waiting for you to invite them into your business. Your job is to find them.

❏ *Practice the THREE-FOOT RULE: Anyone who comes within three feet of you, you ask to join you. Just say, "Would you like to get involved with my company? They've given me the responsibility to build an organization in this area and I would love to know if you'd like to join me?"*

You can call recruiting, "recruiting," or "sponsoring" is fine, too.

Your job in building an organization is to enroll,

recruit or sponsor. Call it what you want. It is important from the beginning in your Network Marketing business, that you let people know the possibilities of moving up the ranks in your company.

❑ Have all of your new recruits focus on becoming management from the time they enroll with you.

❑ Do the 48 hour blitz—ask new recruits who they will sponsor in their first 48 hours! Supersonic growth!

❑ For those who just want to sell the product and make a little extra money—that's fine. It's your responsibility to let them know that the big money is in recruiting. Give people a choice, so they can be the judge.

Here's the close: <u>You</u> just say,

"So, what do you think—do you want to get involved? Is this a good time?

❑ Then, the next step is to ask them to get their checkbook out and write a check to pay for the distributor kit, or to write a check for their initial investment in product inventory.

❑ Start a conversation.

❑ Give your presentation.

❑ Ask a lot of questions.

❑ Stop giving your presentation to unqualified people.

Remember, too, that "No's" come in streaks—and the streaks pass. Add up enough "No's" and they equal a "Yes."

Recruiting is a numbers game. Period.

Here are two powerful questions that you can ask people:

"Would an opportunity to earn some extra money interest you?"

When they answer, "Yes," ask them this:

"Are you willing to invest a little time earning it?"

Of course, when they answer, "Yes" to this question, set an appointment to get together with them to share your opportunity.

One of the biggest misconceptions in Network Marketing is that you personally need to sponsor thousands and thousands of people to make any real money. It's not true.

Most of the time, your first four to five recruits are the hardest to get. It's amazing how inspiring it can be to get just one enthusiastic recruiter into your successline. That seems to bring out the leader in people more than anything else.

You really need three to five strong, directly sponsored representatives, and go three levels deep to become successful.

After you have sponsored those 5 people, you teach them how to sponsor 5 people. Now you have 25. Then you teach those 25 to recruit 5 each—and away you go! Pure MLM!

☐ Run contests.
☐ Get enthusiastic.

☐ Continue to recruit personally; soon you'll have 125 people.

Encourage each of them to get 5 people, and then you have 625.

Encourage those 625 to each get 5 people each and teach them how to do it.

All you're ever doing is to teach people how to do what you already know how to do. Each time you take a step up the ladder, you now know how to do and teach a new achievement to your leaders.

Now you have over 3,000 people!

That is what I did! It works—just *Fire Up!* and do it!

☐ Duplicate your efforts.

☐ Be committed to recruiting, training and leadership.

☐ Set your recruiting goals. Recruiting, recruiting, recruiting! Sponsoring, enrolling.

☐ Practice until you can do it, and you CAN.

☐ Concentrate on helping your personal recruits continue recruiting personally.

☐ At the beginning, you are constantly recruiting first-line, front-line people in order to find at least three to five outstanding leaders. Sometimes you have to recruit as many as 20 or more people before you find those very special people.

☐ When people say, *"I have to think it over . . . I have to talk to my spouse . . . I do not know whether I am going to do this or not,"* just say *"What information do you need so that you can think it over and make a decision?"* - You will find many more objections answers in <u>MLM Nuts $ Bolts</u>.

Here is my favorite quote:

"One of the noblest things a person can do is to plant a small seed, which will grow into a huge tree that will someday give shade to people that he or she will never know."

Plant away. You never know who'll stop and sit in your shade.

❏ Be a great listener.

❏ Ask your people to identify the three people they will pinpoint to help them get started.

When prospects say, *"Yes I'd like to do this,"* learn to say in return, *"The next step is . . ."* and get them involved right away. Then say, *"Welcome to our successline."*

❏ Tell your successline, "I'm not your boss, I'm not your cheerleader, I'm your coach and your team leader."

Success is something you attract.

❏ **You have to work harder on yourself in this business than when you work at your job. When you work on your job, you earn a living. When you work on yourself, you earn a life.**

❏ Develop your gifts.

❏ Develop your vocabulary.

❏ Develop your stories.

❏ Develop your power and your mind.

❏ Do not settle for less than you can be.

❏ Practice developing your skills and abilities

❑   You can't achieve riches by demand—you become wealthy by performance alone.

❑   Get disgusted and it will have a powerful effect on your performance. Some people call this "creative discontent." Say to yourself, *"I've had it,"* and change.

❑   Get the desire to make an annual six-figure income. Want it badly enough to do what is necessary. Do you want it badly enough to do whatever it takes? You have to. It truly is the only way.

Some will and some will not.

Some do and some do not.

If you can believe it, you can achieve it!

Napoleon Hill and Clement Stone said:

"What the mind of man can believe, he can achieve."

Imagine if they had known what a *woman's* belief could accomplish! Dream big, your dreams are going to see you through.

Fire Up!—Just do it!

Set a personal goal to be the top recruiter 3 years in a row.

How to Make the Commitment

❏ GET COMMITTED.
❏ MAKE YOUR COMMITMENT STICK.
Here are some stages you will go through:

•THE "I THOUGHT IT" STAGE:
Is this dream for me? Could I really do that?

•THE "I CAUGHT IT" STAGE:
Get excited! See yourself in it . . . You want everyone to get on your rocket ship and take the ride to the top with you . . . You are so excited you have to tell everyone!!!

•THE "I BOUGHT IT" STAGE:
Put a deposit down on it. Put an investment into it to make it happen. Pay the price. If you're going to capture that dream, make an investment of your time, energy, your dedication, passion and love . . .

Many people quit at this stage. Do you know why? Because they've invested so little, it's easier to quit than it is to stick in there and see it through. A solid investment in yourself will keep it all going.

• THE "I SOUGHT IT" STAGE:
Desire sets in . . . You want it so bad it possesses you. You're willing to give everything you have to be the best you can be. You have **THE WILL TO WIN!** *Your dream is realized and you can say it was* well worth *paying the price!!*

The people who make a personal commitment to work the business are always successful! It's never failed. It will not fail you either.

People who are reluctant to make the commitment never get started. In most cases it's not because the *need* is not present. It's not because there is no *time*—we always make time for the things we want and need. And it's not because there is no *help* available.

In order for you to make a proper commitment, it is essential that you recognize that your plan has been proven to work for anyone who works the plan. Don't let the lack of planning be an excuse for you in the coming months. Realize at the start that your success depends on your personal commitment and planning.

There are many factors that will add to and hasten your success. If you can commit to these nine principles, I guarantee you successful results.

Will you . . .

❏ Have personal written goals and review them every day?

❏ Set a personal example—i.e., do whatever it takes to get the job done?

❏ Concentrate on the opportunity?

❏ Be positive and not allow any negative influences to change your thinking?

❏ Teach others?

❏ Spend a minimum of 50 hours a month building yourself a future?

❏ Make a commitment to work at your business on a spare time basis for at least one year?

❏ Commit to the CANI philosophy of Constant And Never-Ending Improvement?

❏ Persist until you succeed? (The only people who do not succeed in this business are the people who quit.)

Planning and Commitment are your *keys to success.*

To succeed in Network Marketing, you must commit 10 to 15 hours a week to building your business.

You are in control of your success.

Realize your performance and production are dependent solely upon activities that have already been proven to work for thousands and thousands of others.

Get committed. Stay committed. Your dreams are going to see you through.

Fire up! Just do it!!

Fire Way Up!

DESIRE SLEEPS.

You can wake it up by reading one line in a book. You might hear one line in a seminar. One lyric from a song. One piece of dialogue from a movie and it awakens.

☐ Have conversations with friends who will level with you.

☐ Welcome all new experiences.

☐ Let your life touch you. Let life itself move you.

☐ Quit putting up walls. Some walls do keep out disappointments, but they also keep out happiness.

☐ Decision making is powerful. Clean up your decisions. Study and practice how to do this. Indecision is a decision, but indecision is a thief of opportunity. The day you decide, the day that you start to make good decisions, that is the day your life will begin to change for the better forever.

☐ Do not delay. Do not postpone. Resolve: "I will do this now, and I will be the best I can possibly be. I am going to change, I am going to become successful."

☐ See how much your business can grow this year. Have extensive growth on your part.

☐ Devote yourself to personal development, not self-sacrifice. You do not have to have self-sacrifice unless that's what you want. But know that that will earn you contempt. Personal development earns respect.

The best gift you can give to others is your own personal development. If you work on your gifts, you will not have to worry about your promotions. The world will make a place for you. Your company will make a place for you.

☐ Go to work on yourself.

☐ Decide to climb the mountain, to walk away from everything and everybody who will not help you.

☐ Get serious, your dreams are going to see you through.

☐ Words create light, and what happens when all of a sudden someone can't see? It's like you are blind and in the dark. Realize that your words can turn on lights for people. Just flip the power switch to ON—big time. It's just like that, like flipping a switch. Turn on the flood lights—see it. Believe it.

☐ Imagine there are a thousand people in your successline. See it and achieve it. Believe it. If I can do it, don't you think anyone can do it?

Where are you going to be five years from now? That's well into the Twenty-First Century. Get going, come on!

Thank all of you for allowing me to invest in your life.

Ask for God's help. I respect you, I care about you. Just do it and do it now, so that as soon as you can, you can say to your people, "I did it!" That will make such a big difference for them. You have no idea.

Thank you for your time.

Network Marketing is the stuff dreams are made of, and you can do it.

I believe in you.

Stick with it and never, ever give up.
Don't be average, Be a champion,
Be the very best you can be. Go for greatness!
Make your life an unbelievable masterpiece.
Master your moments.
God Bless America—and—may God bless you!
I love you, I need you, you are beautiful.

When you have just one log and you light it (that's you by yourself) there is a small flame; throw another log on the fire and what happens? The flame is bigger and hotter and spreads quicker. Throw another log or two onto those two logs (add more recruits) and what do you get? And then more and more logs, and guess what? All of those logs together become a bonfire! Now, throw tons of passion into that organization and hundreds of thousands of people and watch what happens! It's not just magic, it's reality, your fire is going to spread to others. It all starts with you, just recruit one person and watch the bonfire begin! *Fire Up!*

Fire Up!

Interview with Bill Ruhe (Jan's husband)

I WAS INTRODUCED TO JAN BY A CLIENT OF MINE at a charity party in Dallas. He told me Jan was looking for an attorney to represent her.

Jan was then and is now the most remarkable woman I have ever met. She is sensitive, loving, has ideas of her own and is in very good control of herself. She is a very charismatic leader.

To give Jan some time for her business, I am sometimes the chef, sometimes the chauffeur. I attend meetings with her. I listen to her talk about her business. When she's off on business trips, I'm in touch with her on a daily basis. When she comes home, I'm there to meet her with wine and roses and I always tell her I appreciate her very much.

I feel immense pride about the income that Jan earns. I feel that because she works so diligently at being the best that she can be, she deserves to make the money that she does. It's exciting to be married to a woman who makes an excess of $500,000 a year, and I truly adore her.

Interview with Clayton White (Age 15)-1993

MOM AND I GOT OFF THE AIRPLANE and got into a limo and rode all the way into downtown San Francisco. We did a little shopping and went across the Golden Gate Bridge into Sausalito. It's a sight I had never seen before. We picked out a great hotel that we stayed in and just went shopping all day. It was a lot of fun.

I play sports. Football is my best sport and I play fullback.

In one particular game, we were behind 6-0 and we got down to the two yard line and there were 18 seconds left in the game. We got into a huddle and the quarterback called a play to the fullback. It was a "slant right," which meant that I got the ball.

I went up to the line and I was very nervous. The crowd was really into it. The quarterback said, "Ready . . . go!" and turned around and gave me the ball. I got hit in the backfield and spun out and just fell down in the end zone. Touchdown! Everybody jumped up out on the field and it was a really great experience.

I consider myself a leader and the reason is because when I go out on the football field, the people, my friends, and everybody in the stands are counting on me to make something happen. If I don't make something happen, I don't think anything really will.

The day before one of our football games, two of my friends and I went and watched the movie "Rudy." It was really a motivator. We had never seen it before and I loved it. I went right home and told my mom to go see it. It is a great positive movie. She went with my step-dad and they loved it.

My mother is there for me when I get home from school. I usually get home at 6:00 p.m., because of football practice. When I'm there, we all eat dinner every night as a family and we discuss what's going on in our lives. It's really fun.

You can tell my mother from my friends' moms, because when she walks in the room, you know who she is—because she looks and is a leader.

I have travelled many places with my mother. I've been to the Dominican Republic, Cancun, skiing in Aspen, Vail for the summers, Washington, D.C., Chicago, Virginia, the Caribbean, San Francisco, New Orleans, Nashville, and Hawaii.

Let me tell you about the Dominican Republic at Club Med.

I was in the Dominican Republic and I was in the Kids' Club, because I was only about nine years old. We went up on this hill and there was this big trapeze like in a circus. I was like, "I'm not getting up there." and Mom said, "You go get up there, you need to try new things." I said, "Okay," and went up there and I did it— and I fell. I fell into the nets and it was the first time I had ever done it.

There was another experience like that in

Hawaii—my mother wanted me to go surfing and I really didn't want to go. But she told me I would have fun and I did. I went out and I did it.—my big sister and I, and we just got on surfboards and we just got on surfboards and rode the waves.

In Cancun, I was 13 years old and my curfew was 12:00 midnight, so I had to be up in the room by then. I went out on the beach from 11:00 p.m. to 12:00 and just sat there and looked across the ocean and at all the lights, and it was really a pretty sight. I had never seen it before. Most people do not get to experience what I have experienced through travelling with my mom.

A lucky day is a day when someone takes time to make you feel important, and puts their time in to make your day a better day. I have had a lucky day.

One day, my mother came in and she woke me up and she said, "Today is your lucky day."

I was like "What do you mean?" and she says, "You'll see."

One of my Lucky Days we went to Sound Warehouse and Mom got me three compact discs. We told the people up there that it was my Lucky Day and they responded, "Well, I'm going to call my mother and tell her I need a Lucky Day."

It was pretty funny. Then we went to Boot Town and I got a pair of western boots and a duster and a jacket. We went out to lunch and just had a great time eating and talking about the day and it wound up as one of the best days I have ever had.

My mother is a very important person in my life, because I count on her and she's there whenever I need her. I always know I can count on her and she will be there for me.

By the way, after moving to Aspen, Clayton played fullback and scored eight touchdowns in one football game–as school record as well as a state record! Clayton also broke two other Colorado football records!

Clayton says, "Thank you Mom for never giving up on me," on the song "Never Give Up!" by Jan Ruhe, produced in 1998 (to order, go to www.janruhe.com).

Clayton is presently 20 years old, a sophomore in college in Colorado and the lead singer in a band! He will be transferring to a large university in the south in the fall of 1998.

Interview with Sarah White (Age 17)-1993

I WAS AT MODELING SCHOOL ONE SATURDAY and my parents picked me up on my lunch break to take me out to a restaurant across the street. We were all sitting there eating lunch and, out of the blue, my mom pulled out a couple of cards and handed them to me.

It was a surprise. I didn't know what to think!

The first card said, "Look in card number two for more details." So I opened card number two and it was this poem:

Sarah, something you have said made us all think red.
Because you are so dear, let us make ourselves clear.
We are all so proud of you. Sister Ashley, brother
 Clayton, Mom and Billy Ruhe.
May your senior year be brighter because a big surprise, it
 is special just like you.
However, it is not white and blue.
It is hot red and black, and it is here to stay.
So Sarah doll, you can now drive away.
The rules we will plan together tonight.
Drive safe our darling, Sarah, evermore.
We all love you Sarah, now open your present and run
 out.
It is parked near the front door!

And then they handed me a container, and on the front it said, "Sarah's BMW" and inside were the keys. I started crying.

Everyone in the restaurant was staring at me, and I just kind of stood there. Finally, my family said, "Go out, go out and find your car—it's in the parking lot."

I went out and there was my beautiful car!

My mom makes me feel part of her success, because she is always there for me. She motivates me. We discuss many different topics. She takes me around the country introducing me to people. It truly makes me feel as if I am a part of her success.

My mom is home for me every day when I get home from school, and this is special because I get home about 2:00 p.m. every day, and my brother and sister don't get home until much later and we just have share-time together. We discuss all the events of the day.

I feel like a leader because I have contributed a lot to my school and to my community. I've participated in many activities. I have page-long list of things I have done—such as cheerleading, drill team, volunteer work.

My mom has instilled many values in me that I look for in my relationships, such as trust, dependability, responsibility.

I've been to many seminars over the years. I've been to see and hear Tom Hopkins and Jim Rohn. I have listened to Anthony Robbins and they have all been mentors in my life. They've helped me immensely with my communication skills.

My mom has taken me on many trips. We've been to Mexico, England, Canada, Hawaii, the Caribbean, Africa, snow skiing in Aspen, New Mexico, summers in

Vail, all over the United States. When I was in Hawaii, I had a private surf coach and I went scuba diving.

I have many special memories that I will cherish for a lifetime.

When I graduated from high school, my GPA was 3.8 I think a lot of this has to do with my mom's encouragement and positive attitude. I was accepted at SMU and studied communications and marketing. I plan to use these degrees towards Network Marketing and motivational speaking. While at SMU, I published several feature articles for the SMU student newspaper and pledged Delta Gamma Society.

After my first year at SMU, I decided to transfer to Colorado University in Boulder to be closer to our new mountain home. My first summer in Colorado, I got a great job as an intern for channel KSPN, reporting the news in Aspen. At CU, my first semester there, I became the news anchor for CU and reported the news every morning.

In late 1995, I was accepted to the Semester at Sea program. I joined 450 American students to go around the world, studying on a cruise ship and stopping at 11 ports of call. We began in the Bahamas and stopped in Venezuela, Brazil, South Africa, Kenya, India, Vietnam, The Philippines, Hong Kong, Japan, and ended in Seattle, Washington. The great news is that my mother and sister met me in Kenya to go on a safari with me to celebrate my 20th birthday! In December, 1997, I graduated from CU. I completed college in 3 1/2 years.

Sarah is presently 22 years old and living in Louisiana. She is currently involved in building her own Network Marketing business.

Interview with Ashley White (Age 13)-1993

MY MOM TAKES ME ON A LOT OF TRIPS. We have been to Hawaii many times. Mom and I went to Maui once by ourselves, and that was a special trip. I am involved with soccer, volleyball, modeling, basketball, and I take piano lessons. My mom comes to every single one of my games.

I consider myself a leader because my mom always talks about my being a leader and I believe her. I get myself fired up at my soccer games by doing a cheer called "Fire Up!" and it just helps me play better when I go on the field. My teammates get fired up too by the cheer before we go out to play and we all seem to play better.

After moving to Aspen, Ashley joined the Aspen Ski Club, and now 17 years old in high school is an outstanding varsity soccer player and varsity cheerleader.

She was named the #1 top varsity cheerleader of Aspen High School her Junior year. By the time she graduates from high school, Ashley will have lettered five times in sports.

About the Author

JAN RUHE was born in St. Petersburg, Florida, raised in Calallen, Texas and graduated from Texas Tech University in Lubbock, Texas in 1970, with a B.A. in Sociology. She first married in 1972. Jan has three children, Sarah, Clayton, and Ashley.

Jan joined her Network Marketing company, in 1980, while expecting her third child.

In 1986, Jan and her first husband divorced in a custody battle trial by jury. Jan won and received custody of the children, but in the process, Jan's debts mounted to over $100,000.

Jan began to study the Network Marketing pros in 1985 and has invested thousands of dollars into improving herself. She became a student of Tom Hopkins and Jim Rohn.

By the end of 1990, Jan had completely paid off her debts and married Bill Ruhe, one of her attorneys in the child custody case. In 1993, she published her first book, <u>Pour Yourself a Cup of Ambition</u>, a combination of her personal story in detail and notes from her private journals. She sold 1,000 copies of her book in the first ten days. It is no longer in print. The contents of this book are now in <u>MLM Nuts & Bolts</u>.

Jan has trained over 25,000 people in her career and has personally sponsored over 500 representatives into her company. She has reached the top position in her company. She is a Diamond Sales Director, and her total organization numbered over 7,000 people in 1997. By the summer of 1995, Jan Ruhe was named an American millionaire. In 1997, Jan published the MLM best selling "How to" training manual—<u>MLM Nuts $ Bolts</u> as well as the Fire Up! music which includes two songs — "*It's Up to You*," and "*Never Give Up.*"

Jan was featured in the September 1997 issue of *Working at Home* magazine, published by *Success* magazine. She has also been featured in *Money Makers Monthly*, and in 1998, she became a member of Tom Hopkins faculty and is a Master for Upline®. In 1998, Jan was interviewed to possibly be featured on the *Oprah Winfrey Show*. Jan now speaks and trains sales forces all over the world.

Jan's life purpose is to share her success with you, so that you can become a leader in your business. She believes simply, if she can do it, so can you. As she will tell you:

"*Just say, 'Put me in, Coach—I'm ready to play! . . . I'm ready to play today!' You make constant achievements when you fire up. Just get busy, starting right now, and make your life the incredible masterpiece it's meant to be. Master each moment on Earth. There are angels watching over you. You were created to succeed. Fire up big time and just do it!*"

As her close friend, I ask you to trust and believe her, I do.

—John Milton Fogg

For those of you who want THE actual words to the *Fire Up!* music, here they are:

Fire Up! (say it 9 times)
Don't you know your life is up to you?
Ignite or melt, the choice is yours, you are the switch that opens doors!
Turn it on, turn it on, turn it on!
When you do what others won't, you will get what others don't!
Turn it on, turn it on, turn it on!
Fire Up! (say it 9 times)
Don't you know your life is up to you?
Fan the flames of your fire, with every dream that you desire,
Turn it on, turn it on, turn it on!
Flip that switch, ignite, inspire, throw tons of passion on your fire!
Throw it on, throw it on, throw it on!
Fire Up! (say it 9 times)
It's up to you, it's up to you, know what to do?
Keep burnin', burnin', burnin'
Every time you throw a log on the fire, it's up to you, you know what to do
Every dream that you desire, fuels your passion, fuels your fire!
Turn it on, turn it on, turn it on! It's up to you!
Fire Up! (say it 9 times)
It's up to who? It's up to you
Fire Up!
So what can you do?
Turn it on, turn it on, turn it on! Ignite your passion, no one can do it for you!
It's up to who? It's up to you!
Fire Up!
Go for it, Big time—Fire Up!
Ignite that passion, ignite it and Fire Up! Fire WAY up!
Ignite it!
Fire Up!

Music written by Jan Ruhe, David Bluefield, and John Fogg

Be a Winner

Winners make commitments.

> *Losers* make promises they can't or won't keep.

Winners proclaim, "I'm good, but I can do better."

> *Losers* claim, "I'm no worse than a lot of others."

Winners get to the source of the problems.

> *Losers* side-step the issues, but never really get around them.

Winners admit, "I was wrong."

> *Losers* say, "It wasn't my fault."

Winners look for a better way.

> *Losers* accept the way that it is.

Winners learn from the leaders.

> *Losers* attempt to discredit the leaders.

What do you need to work on to *Fire Up?*

❑

❑

❑

❑

❑

❑

❑

❑

❑

❑

❑

What do you need to work on to *Fire Up?*

❑

❑

❑

❑

❑

❑

❑

❑

❑

❑

❑

What do you need to work on to *Fire Up?*

❑

❑

❑

❑

❑

❑

❑

❑

❑

❑

❑

What do you need to work on to *Fire Up?*

❑

❑

❑

❑

❑

❑

❑

❑

❑

❑

❑

Lightning Source UK Ltd.
Milton Keynes UK
UKOW030215240712

196448UK00001B/8/P